Henry Purcell

Ten Duets

edited by Timothy Roberts

CONTENTS

Book one (ISBN 0 85249 492 0)
   1. We the spirits of the air 3
   2. Two daughters of this aged stream are we 7
   3. Shepherd, shepherd, leave decoying 12
   4. My dearest, my fairest 14
   5. Sound the trumpet 20
   6. Lost is my quiet for ever 25

Book two (ISBN 0 85249 519 6)
   7. No, resistance is but vain 2
   8. O Dive custos 11
   9. Hark! how the songsters of the grove 23
  10. Let Caesar and Urania live 28

STAINER & BELL LTD
23 Gruneisen Road, London N3 ID2

© 1979 Stainer & Bell Ltd

INTRODUCTION

Alfred Moffat's edition of six vocal duets by Purcell was published by Augener in 1901. Containing some of Purcell's most immediately attractive music, the selection proved to be of enduring popularity. The first book of the present edition comprises those same six duets in completely revised form, while the second book contains a further selection of four more extended duets intended to complete a fuller picture of Purcell's mastery of the idiom.

The edition As an anthology for practical performance, it is not the purpose of this edition to untangle the web of extant sources. None of the duets in Book one survive in the composer's autograph or in an edition known to have been supervised by him. The present edition is based on *Orpheus Britannicus* together with selected early manuscript sources, listed at the end of each duet. For a description of the sources the reader is referred to F. B. Zimmerman's *Henry Purcell: An Analytical Catalogue of His Music* (Macmillan, 1963). Zimmerman's catalogue numbers are given at the head of each piece.

For the sake of legibility the realizations are printed full size, except where notes have been added below the original bass line. Other editorial additions are printed small, with the exception of ties, which are distinguished by a small vertical stroke. Cautionary accidentals are placed in brackets. The bass is sparsely and inconsistently figured in the sources, what figures there are generally indicating no more than the movement of the voice parts; no figures are given here. $\frac{2}{2}$ has been substituted for the time signature ₵. Some of the duets have been transposed; details are given in the Notes at the end of each. Vocal ranges are indicated at the beginning of each piece, together with the original voice allocations and feasible alternatives in brackets. Textual spelling and punctuation have been modernized.

Performance Some application of stylistically appropriate ornamentation can enhance this music greatly. Ornaments are scarce in the sources, and some editorial trills and divisions have been added to the vocal parts as a guide; however, singers should be encouraged to use their own aptitude and imagination in that matter. Ornamentation is most appropriate at cadences and in repeated sections. Much of Purcell's vocal writing includes florid passages that attempt to notate the improvized graces of seventeenth-century singers: see, for instance, the appoggiaturas and slides in no. **6**. Such notated ornaments should be sung with a certain rhythmic freedom and spontaneity.

Singers should be aware of the mid-Baroque conventions of inequality and overdotting. The dot in this music rarely has its exact modern meaning; it can just as easily indicate a triplet rhythm (especially in slow or lyrical pieces) or a sharp, overdotted one (particularly in triumphant or majestic music). Similarly, pairs of quavers (or crotchets in a minim beat) may often be performed unequally, usually with the first note longer than second. (Combining these conventions, try performing no. **6** with the dotted crotchets overdotted, the dotted quavers underdotted and the even quavers unequal; the result will be a subtly varied $\frac{9}{8}$ rhythm.) The 'scotch snap'—semiquaver-dotted quaver—is often appropriate in English music, and will often be suggested by the natural rhythm of the words.

No dynamics have been added to the vocal parts, but those suggested in the keyboard part may be taken by the singers as a starting point. However, the idea of 'terraced dynamics' should be avoided in this music; changes of tone colour and articulation will be found more telling than extremes of dynamics.

The realizations are conceived primarily in terms of the harpsichord, though they may easily be adapted for the piano or chamber organ. In all but the smallest rooms the harpsichord should be reinforced by a cello, bassoon or viola da gamba on the bass. Pianists should never allow the bass to become mere background, nor allow the right hand to obscure the voices. Players with some feel for the style may adapt the accompaniment freely; some variation is especially desirable in repeats.

Acknowledgements Thanks are due to the librarians of the Royal Academy of Music, the Royal College of Music and the British Library for granting access to their collections.

London, 1978   TIMOTHY ROBERTS

1. WE THE SPIRITS OF THE AIR

Z.630/17

John Dryden

Henry Purcell

© Copyright 1979 by Stainer & Bell Ltd

10
-cays, great-ness clogg'd with scorn de-cays, With the slave no
clogg'd with scorn de-cays, with scorn de-cays, With the slave
15
tr
em-pire, no, no, no, no, no, no em-pire stays.
tr
no em-pire, no, no, no, no, no em-pire stays.
20
We the spi-rits of the air, That of hu-man things take
We the spi-rits of the air, That of hu-man things take
f

care,__ Out of__ pi - ty__ now__ de - scend To fore -
care, Out of pi - ty__ now__ de - scend To fore -
-warn__ what__ does__ at - tend. Cease to lan - guish then_ in__
-warn what__ does at - tend. Cease to lan - guish, cease to lan - guish then_ in__
vain, Since ne-ver, ne-ver, ne - ver, ne-ver, ne - - ver__
vain, Since ne-ver, ne-ver, ne - ver, ne-ver, ne - - ver__

Notes From *The Indian Queen*, Act III, where it is preceded by the duet 'O how happy are we' and followed by the solo song 'I attempt from love's sickness to fly'. The refrain is sung there by a chorus with string accompaniment, but here the piece is given as a duet, in which form it appears in *Orpheus Britannicus*. Moffat gave it new words, 'Let us wander not unseen', adapted from Milton's *L'Allegro*; in this edition the original text is restored. Supernatural grace and charm are called for in the gavotte-like refrain, the other verses perhaps needing to be more sustained and lyrical. Original key A minor.

Sources British Library Add. MSS 31447 (*c.* 1700), 31449 (after 1696) and 31453 (early 18th century); *Orpheus Britannicus*, 1721.

2. TWO DAUGHTERS OF THIS AGED STREAM

Z.628/29

John Dryden
Henry Purcell

15
sea - green locks have combed, and both our sea - green locks have combed, have
both our sea-green locks have combed for ye, and both our sea-green locks have
combed for ye. Come, come, come, come, bathe with us an
tr
combed for ye. Come, come, bathe with us an
p
20
hour or two, Come, come, come, come
hour or two, Come, come, come, come

25
na - ked in for we are so, What dan - ger,
na - ked in for we are so, What
f
what dan - ger from a na - ked foe?
dan - ger from a na - ked foe?
30
Come, come, bathe with us,
Come, come, come, come, bathe with us,
p

Come, come, bathe and share What pleasures in the floods appear. We'll beat the waters till they bound, we'll beat the waters

Notes From *King Arthur,* Act IV. Seductiveness is the key-note here, though it should be subtle to match Purcell's delightful musical imagery. Take particular care over the intonation of the diminished fourths on 'come, come'. The canonic entries from bar 37 to the end should be very clear; note that the bass is finally given some thematic significance at bar 45.

Sources British Library Add. MS 31447 (*c.* 1700); Royal Academy of Music MS 21 (1698-9); *Orpheus Britannicus,* 1721 and *c.*1745

3. SHEPHERD, SHEPHERD, LEAVE DECOYING

Z.628/16b

John Dryden
Henry Purcell

© Copyright 1979 by Stainer & Bell Ltd

Notes From *King Arthur*, Act II. The piece is first played as a ritornello by oboes and recorders and then sung by two boys. The words demand a light pastoral tone, though perhaps not without a touch of irony. A little variation is possible on the repeats, but do not add anything that would be out of place in Arcady. The tempo is lively but not too fast to allow the tone to fill out a little on the melismas in the second half. Original key G minor.

Bar 8: 'shot' = payment, 'especially at a tavern or for entertainment' (*OED*).

Sources British Library Add. MS 31447 (c. 1700); Royal Academy of Music MS 21 (1698-9).

4. MY DEAREST, MY FAIREST

Z.585/2

?Norton

Daniel (?) Purcell

© Copyright 1979 by Stainer & Bell Ltd

15
1
– – – – guish, I lan – guish for you. My
– – – – guish, I lan – guish for you.
2
20
you. Thy kind – ness has won — me,
you. Thy charm — has un – done — me, I
f
25
I ne'er, — no, ne'er shall be free.
ne'er, — I ne'er, — no, ne'er shall be free. I
p

faint___ with the plea-sure I__ fain would__ re-peat, Ah,

why are__ love's__ rap-tures so short and so__ sweet? Thus

press - ing, thus press - ing and kiss - ing, fresh

And kiss - ing, thus press - ing and kiss - ing, fresh

40
joys we'll pur - sue, And e - ver be hap - py, and
joys we'll pur - sue, And e - ver be hap - py, and
e - ver be true, and e - ver be
e - ver be true, and e - ver be
45
hap - py, and e - ver be true. But a - las! should you
hap - py, and e - ver be true.
f

50
change,
No, ne - ver, my
Ah, tell me not so!
55
dear - est,
no, no,
No, ne - ver, my fair - est,
no, no,
60
no, no, no,
no, no, no, my
no,
no, no, no, no, no, no, my

Notes From *Pausanias*, the incidental music to which was completed after Purcell's death by his brother Daniel. It is not certain exactly who composed this fine Italianate duet; it is attributed to Henry in the first published source but to Daniel in a contemporary MS. The flowing triple time is typical of the *bel canto* style (compare the famous duet that concludes Monteverdi's *L'incoronazione di Poppea*). The vocal lines must not drag, and the melody should pass smoothly between them, though bars 47–55 can be more declamatory. The second part was written for a baritone, but may be taken by a male alto. The first time bar is editorial, the repeat being suggested in I.595.6 by an undotted double bar. Original key A minor.

Sources British Library I.595.6 (single sheet, *c.* 1700); *Orpheus Britannicus, c.* 1745.

5. SOUND THE TRUMPET

Z.323/3

Henry Purcell

sound the trum-pet, sound,— sound,—
trum - pet, sound the trum - pet,sound,— sound,—
10
sound— the trum-pet till a - round—
sound— the trum-pet till a - round— You make the
You make the list' - ning shores re -
list' - ning shores re - bound,— you make the

-bound, re - bound, the list' - ning_shoresre -
list'-ning shores re - bound, re-bound, the list' - ning_shores re-
tr
15
1
2
-bound.
-bound.
-bound.
-bound. On the
p
f
On the spright - - ly haut-boy, the
spright - - ly haut-boy, the spright-ly haut - boy play, the

23

Notes From *Come Ye Sons of Art,* Queen Mary's 1694 birthday ode, where it is sung in D by two countertenors. It appeared in *Orpheus Britannicus* in G; the latter version is here transposed down a tone, with some alterations introduced from the original version. This is a virtuoso piece, but do not be tempted to take it too fast. Purcell has set each section of the text in a different key, and this might be matched by changes of vocal colour. 'Hautboy' should be pronounced 'ho-boy' or simply 'oboe'. The implied irregular barring in bars 27–28 has been indicated by dashes.

Sources Royal College of Music MS 993 (1765); *Orpheus Britannicus,* 1721.

6. LOST IS MY QUIET FOR EVER

Z.502

Henry Purcell

15
Lost is life's hap - pi-est part, Lost all,
Lost is life's hap - pi - est part, Lost
20
all, all my ten - der en - dea - vours To
all, all my ten - der en - dea - vours To
25
touch an in -
touch an in -

27

-sen-si-ble heart. heart. But though my de-spair is past cu-ring,

-sen-si-ble heart. heart. But though my de-spair is past cu-ring, but though my de-spair is past cu-ring,

but though my de-spair, my de-spair is past cu-ring, And much un-de-served is my fate, I'll

though my de-spair is past cu-ring, but though my de-spair is past cu-ring, And much un-de-served is my fate,

Notes A piece of exceptional intensity, in which the strong accents that fall naturally on each first beat must not detract from the overall shape of the phrases. Try to feel bars 1–16 and 17–27 as single spans, and find a tempo at which the repeat does not make the piece too long. The second half could be made more intense by swelling through the held dotted minims, to bring out the suspensions. Original key signature two flats.

Sources British Library MS Eg. 2960 (late 17th century); *The Banquet of Music*, vol. 5 (1691); *Orpheus Britannicus*, 1721